Do You Really Want a Cat?

Bridget Heos • Illustrated by Katya Longhi

amicus
illustrated

amicus illustrated

Amicus Illustrated is published by Amicus
P.O. Box 1329, Mankato, MN 56002
www.amicuspublishing.us

Library of Congress Cataloging-in-Publication Data
Heos, Bridget.
 Do you really want a cat? / by Bridget Heos ; illustrated by Katya Longhi.
     pages cm. — (Do you really want— ?)
 Includes bibliographical references.
 Summary: "A mischievous cat (and the narrator) teach a young girl the
responsibility—and the joys—of owning a cat. Includes 'Is this pet right for me?'
quiz"—Provided by publisher.
 ISBN 978-1-60753-203-3 (library binding) — ISBN 978-1-60753-396-2 (ebook)
 1. Cats—Juvenile literature. I. Longhi, Katya, illustrator. II. Title.
 SF445.7.H463 2014
 636.8—dc23
                                    2012035929

Editor: Rebecca Glaser
Designer: The Design Lab

Printed in the United States of America at Corporate Graphics
in North Mankato, Minnesota.

Date 9/2014 PO 1229

10 9 8 7 6 5 4

About the Author

Bridget Heos is the author of more than
40 books for children and teens, including
What to Expect When You're Expecting Larvae
(2011, Lerner). She lives in Kansas City with
husband Justin, sons Johnny, Richie, and
J.J., plus a dog, cat, and Guinea pig.
You can visit her online at
www.authorbridgetheos.com.

About the Illustrator

Katya Longhi was born in southern Italy.
She studied illustration at the Nemo NT
Academy of Digital Arts in Florence. She loves
to create dream worlds with horses, flying
dogs, and princesses in her illustrations.
She currently lives in northern Italy
with her Prince Charming.

So you say you want a cat.
You really, really want a cat.
**But do you *really*
want a cat?**

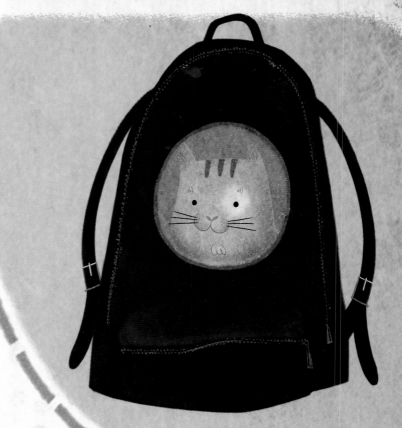

If you have a cat, you'll need
to feed her and give her
water—twice a day at least.
If you forget...

… she'll track down her own meals. Actually, she might do this anyway. Cats like to hunt! But eating animals can give them tummy aches.

It's as if they can sense my arrival!

Fasten her collar with a bell. That way, birds and mice will hear her coming.

But maybe you won't need
a bell. You have a decision
to make. Will your cat
be allowed outside?
The outdoors has sunlight
and grass and birds.

But it also has cars and dogs and feral (wild) cats. An older cat may be used to roaming. If you let her wander, make sure she comes in at night. Nothing good happens after 8 p.m.

If she's a kitten, she'll be happy inside.
She won't know what "outside" is!
You'll need to keep her busy, though.

Do you like to play hide-and-seek?

Do you like to toss a toy mouse?

Do you think chasing crumpled paper is fun?

Your kitten will! But she'll want somebody to play with!

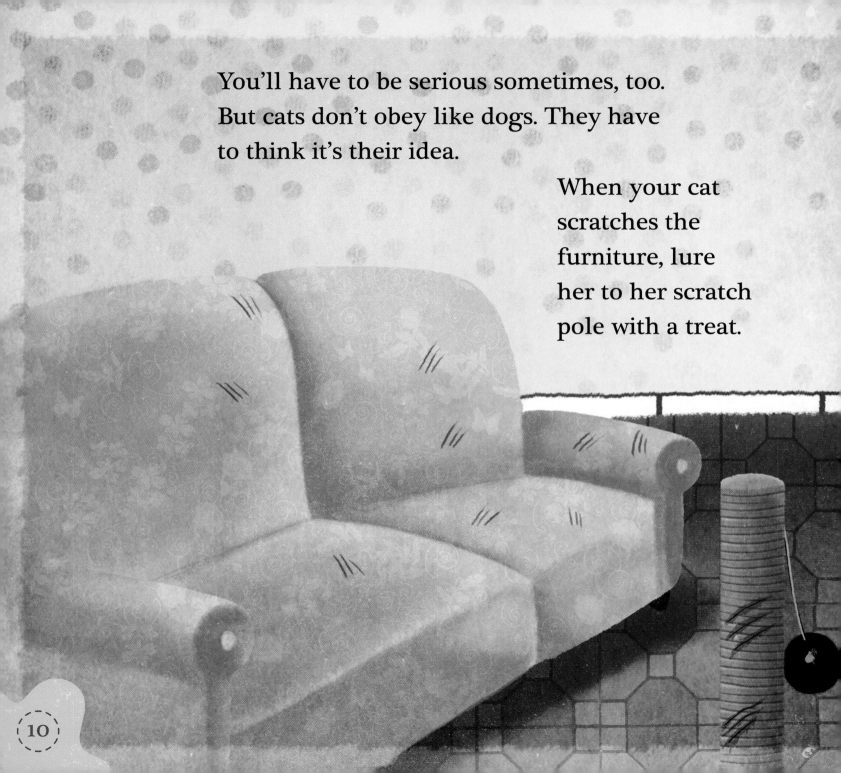

You'll have to be serious sometimes, too.
But cats don't obey like dogs. They have
to think it's their idea.

When your cat
scratches the
furniture, lure
her to her scratch
pole with a treat.

If your cat eats plants, spray the leaves with vinegar.

If she jumps on the kitchen counter,
spray her lightly with water.
But don't drench poor kitty!

The cat will bathe herself, but you'll need to help her with some things.

Take her to the vet.

Comb her fur.
Clean her litter box.

If you don't…

... it will stink, and she will not be happy!

Lastly, you'll want to
snuggle with your cat.
But don't grab her.

If you do...

... she may scratch or bite.

Snuggling has to be her idea!

But cat snuggles
are worth the wait!

So if you don't mind cleaning her litter box, and if you're willing to feed her and comb her fur, then maybe you do want a cat.

Now I have a question for the cat.
You say you want a person.
You really, really want a person.

But do you *really* want a person?

QUIZ

Is this the right pet for me?

Should you get a kitten or older cat? An inside or outside cat? And which breed is right for you? Take this quiz to get an idea. (Be sure to talk to breeders or shelter volunteers, too!)

1. Do you have lots of time to play with your cat?
2. Do you live far away from busy streets?
3. Are the other animals in your neighborhood friendly?
4. Are you willing to groom your cat's fur?

If you answered . . .

a. YES TO ALL FOUR QUESTIONS, you can choose almost any type of cat.
b. NO TO NUMBER ONE, you should choose an adult cat that is less playful.
c. NO TO NUMBER TWO OR THREE, choose an indoor cat. You'll need to play with her inside to keep her busy!
d. YES TO NUMBER FOUR, you can get a longhair breed, such as a Persian or Maine Coon. If you answered no, choose a shorthair breed, such as an American shorthair.

Websites

ASPCA Kids
http://www.aspca.org/aspcakids/
A site including games, videos, and photos that educates
children about pet care, animal issues, and animal careers,
sponsored by the American Society for the Prevention of
Cruelty to Animals.

Cat Care, Behavior Tips:
The Humane Society of the United States
http://www.humanesociety.org/animals/cats/
The Humane Society offers advice on playing with your cat,
adopting a cat, bringing a new cat home, and much more.

Cat Guide: Cat Source: Animal Planet
http://animal.discovery.com/cat-guide/
Learn how to train your cat to use a litter box and get
answers to questions about your cat's health and more.

It's My Life: Family: Pets from PBSKids
http://pbskids.org/itsmylife/family/pets/
This site from PBSKids offers information about choosing a
pet and the responsibilities that go along with having pets.

Tama and Friends visit Petfinder.com
http://www.petfinder.com/tama//index.html
The kids' section of Petfinder.com offers games,
pet tips, pet listings, and a section for parents.

Read More

Head, Honor.
Cats. Pets Plus.
Smart Apple Media, 2013.

Hoare, Ben.
Owning a Pet Cat. Owning a Pet.
Sea-to-Sea Publications, 2008.

Huseby, Victoria.
Cat. Looking at Life Cycles.
Smart Apple Media, 2009.

Johnson, Jinny.
Cats and Kittens. Get to Know Your Pet.
Smart Apple Media, 2009.

Rau, Dana Meachen.
Top 10 Cats for Kids.
Enslow Elementary, 2009.

Meow.